# THE DOWNWARD ASCENT

EDNA HONG

AUGSBURG PUBLISHING HOUSE • MINNEAPOLIS

*THE DOWNWARD ASCENT*



*Library of Congress Catalog Card No. 78-66942*

*International Standard Book No. 0-8066-1679-2*



MANUFACTURED IN THE UNITED STATES OF AMERICA

# CONTENTS

PREFACE 9

ACKNOWLEDGMENTS 11

1

INVITATION TO A SELF-SEEING 13

2

HORIZONTAL EVASIONS OF SELF-SEEING 25

3

VERTICAL EVASIONS OF SELF-SEEING 37

4

DEAD-END DESCENTS 53

5

THE SELF AT THE FOOT OF THE CROSS 67

6

THE EASTERING ASCENT 79

Nowhere, neither in heaven or on earth or in any human relationship, is there a levitation such as is mine when, humbled and ashamed, I turn from my best deed as from something inferior and find rest in *grace*. Let the proud pagan storm heaven or at least try to: from this descent into humility comes the levitation which blissfully arrives at heaven.

SØREN KIERKEGAARD
*Judge for Yourself!*

One cannot study the condition of man without being touched by the plight of man. Though biologically intact, man is essentially afflicted with a sense of helplessness, discontent, inferiority, fear. Outwardly Homo sapiens may pretend to be satisfied and strong; inwardly he is poor, needy, vulnerable, always on the verge of misery, prone to suffer mentally and physically. Scratch his skin and you come upon bereavement, affliction, uncertainty, fear, and pain. Disparity between his appearance and reality is a condition of social integration. Suppressions are the price he pays for being accepted in society. Adjustment involves assenting to odd auspices, conscious of conscience, inevitable hypocrisies. It is, indeed, often "a life of quiet desperation."

ABRAHAM J. HESCHEL
*Who Is Man?*

Deep, deep, and still deep and deeper must we go if we would find out the heart of a man; descending into which is as descending a spiral stair in a shaft, without any end, and where that endlessness is only concealed by the spiralness of the stair, and the blackness of the shaft.

HERMAN MELVILLE
*Pierre*

Redemption is meaningless unless there is cause for it in the actual life we live, and for the last few centuries there has been operating in our culture the secular belief that there is no such cause.

FLANNERY O'CONNOR
"The Fiction Writer and His Country"

# PREFACE

Once in a blue moon a book asks to be written. This seems to be one. As a matter of wry fact, it may be the quixotic fruit of two remarks I overheard.

One I overheard myself making a year or two ago. In our local weekly newspaper I sometimes see an announcement of the meeting of a group of women calling themselves "Women A'glow." Upon seeing this announcement, I without fail think of Augustine pondering God and humanity some 1600 years ago: "What is that which gleams through me and smites my heart without wounding it? I am both a'shudder and a'glow. A'shudder insofar as I am unlike it and a'glow insofar as I am like it."

Somewhat flippantly, I confess, I once made the remark that I planned to organize a group of women who would meet at the same hour on the same day, and we would call ourselves "Women A'shudder." I, of course, had no serious intention of doing so, but neither did I intend to write a book, and here it is. If after reading it you still cannot see any connection between the book and my flippant remark, then either you or I will somehow have failed.

The other overheard remark was made by a clergyman at the beginning of the Lenten season, and he was not being flippant. "When the liturgical year comes up for reform," he said, "I surely hope that Lent will be drastically shortened. Lent is far too long. A long Lent may have served a good purpose in the Middle Ages, but not in our modern times."

Not being quick at retorts and repartee, I have taken two years to think through my answer.

This book is addressed to women (and men, too) who have dropped the a'shudder dimension out of their lives (I shall not organize a "Women A'shudder" group). And to that clergyman or anyone else who thinks that Lent is far too long.

# ACKNOWLEDGMENTS

The author wishes to express her gratitude for permission to reprint material from the following sources:

Brother Antoninus (William O. Everson): *The Crooked Lines of God.* Copyright © 1960 by the University of Detroit Press.

Walker Percy: *Love in the Ruins.* Copyright © 1971 by Farrar, Straus & Giroux. Reprinted by permission of the author.

Josephine W. Johnson: *The Inland Island.* Copyright © 1969 by Josephine Johnson. Published by Simon and Schuster.

Robert Drake: *Flannery O'Connor: A Critical Essay.* Copyright © 1966 by Wm. B. Eerdmans Publishing Co.

Flannery O'Connor: "The Fiction Writer and His Country," from *The Living Novel,* edited by Granville Hicks. Copyright © 1957 by Macmillan Publishing Co., Inc.

Saul Bellow: *Henderson the Rain King.* Copyright © 1958, 1959 by Saul Bellow. Published by The Viking Press, Inc.

Abraham J. Heschel: *Who Is Man?* Copyright © 1965 by Stanford University Press.

Clarence Day: *God and My Father*. Copyright © 1934 by Alfred A. Knopf, Inc.

E. M. Cioran: *The Temptation to Exist,* tr. by Richard Howard. Copyright © 1956 by Librairie Gallimard; English translation © 1968 by Quadrangle / The New York Times Book Co.

Jack Clemo: *The Map of Clay*. Copyright © 1961 by Eyre Methuen Ltd., London. By permission of the author.

Bruce Marshall: *Vespers in Vienna*. Copyright © 1947 by Bruce Marshall. Published by Houghton Mifflin Company, The Riverside Press.

# INVITATION TO A SELF-SEEING

## 1

My ardent and joyful faith, the *Hallelujah* that sings within me, and my disgust with and distrust of myself, my unlovely self, are both truths about me.

In saying this, I catch my unlovely self thinking, "What a lovely thing to say! Is there an audience to hear me say this lovely-sounding truth?"

Thereupon my lovely self thinks, "What a dreadful thing to think at the very moment I am saying such a lovely truth! I hope to heaven nobody heard me thinking it!"

Direct revelations visit me quite frequently—that is, direct revelations about myself from within myself. Perhaps the one that startled me most (not because of the nature of the revelation, for by now the message has become trite, but because of the nature of the occasion) was the sudden unveiling of myself to myself the night of the dinner party when my right arm was severely burned. Sparing you the horrendous details, may I say only that, due to my own carelessness, the burner under the fondue pot exploded and the long sleeve of my blouse caught fire. My husband and the guests beat out the flames, but not before the skin of my entire arm was fit only to be sloughed. I threw my arms, the roasted one and the unroasted, around my husband.

"Oh, Howard!" I wailed—not in pain, although it was agony such as I had never known. Compared to burn pains, birth pains are indulgent as an old-fashioned grandmother. No, this wail came from a woman's natural distress at having spoiled an otherwise delightful occasion.

"Oh, Howard! I spoiled your party!"

And then came the revelation! A purely private one, to me and to no one else. In that agony such as I had never known, something within me whispered, "Beautiful! What noble words! And at such a time! How utterly self-denying!"

And I said it again!

"Oh, Howard! I spoiled your party!"

In other words, my self does not live in a sweet, sunny, one-story rambler but in an old ancestral Gothic house of many floors and rooms and hallways, of dark passageways and spiral staircases, of damp and gloomy cellars and cellarages. The maze of subterranean corridors go downdowndown and eventually converge in one dizzily winding and descending path that dead-ends at the Room of Riddle, the Fall, Original Sin, Original Guilt.

"Back down the slough/To Adam's sin-burnt calcinated bones," wrote the poet Brother Antoninus in "The Making of the Cross." And if there are those who say that the Book of Genesis is a rather flimsy basis for such a riddled room, I would retort: Go ahead and wave your wand of mythology all you want. You cannot get rid of that room. It stands firmly on the bedrock of ethical, spiritual, and psychological experience. Or, to be less pretentious, on the bedrock of plain common sense.

In yet other words: I am sewing my life with a thread that snags and snarls and tangles and knots in the sewing. Get another thread? A better quality? There is no other! The thread with which I sew my life is spun out of the subtle knot that is my human self. "The subtle knot that makes us man," said John Donne in the 17th century. "The knot in which heaven and earth are interlaced," said Abraham J. Heschel in the 20th century.

The 18th and 19th centuries, heady with the New Science, hoped to perfect human nature. "We need nothing to explain human behavior but the laws of physics and chemistry," said the New Science. But if the 20th century has done anything, it has confirmed the knot, confirmed that human nature is far more complex than our puny understanding of it. It has established beyond any doubt that human beings are not perfectible and that they are their own worst problem. As the century of Dachau,

Lidice, Hiroshima, Vietnam, Nigeria, etc. winds down, I can say with truth more well-grounded than ever before in human history that I am sewing my life with a snagging thread spun out of the subtle knot that makes me human.

The knot that makes us human is the joining within us of body and spirit, the finite and the infinite, time and eternity. Modern theologians call this joining a paradox—and sometimes make so much of paradox that one suspects it is a new idolatry. G. K. Chesterton, who refused to be intimidated by a word or to idolize it, said a paradox is simply a truth standing on its head waving its legs to attract our attention.

The Christian doctrine of the dual nature of man is such a truth, and whether it stands on its legs or on its head, it is a mystery beyond our intellect, a knot we cannot untie. At least my poor intellect cannot. Yet everything within and without me tells me it is so. I am more than what you see, and the blackest lie you can tell about me is that I am no more than what you see and that when I die *I am at the end of my nature*.

I am body and spirit. My body hungers for food, thirsts for water, craves the finite, and all its urges are me-centered. My body seeks what is here below. My spirit hungers for Spirit, thirsts for living waters, craves the infinite, and all its urges are God-centered. It seeks eternal ascension. If my body loses its normal appetites, it is sick. If my spirit loses its normal appetites, it, too, is sick. If the body develops abnormal appetites, it can become addicted to self-indulgences, be they food, tobacco, drugs, whatever. If the spirit develops abnormal appetites, it, too, can seek to indulge itself and can become addicted to religious sensations and emotions. It can experience spiritual binges and get spiritual diarrhea and spiritual hangovers. (I never cease to be startled by what Meister Eckhart said in the 14th century—that those who seek spiritual experience *for the sake of spiritual experience* are guilty of spiritual unchastity!) A healthy body can house a sick spirit. A sick body can house a robust spirit. A sick spirit in a sick body—no misery is comparable!

Two worlds within me! Staggering doctrine! *In me* two worlds meet—the world of eternity, infinity, and spirit, and the world of time, finitude, and flesh. That the two worlds must live in tension is obvious, for the one is all on the side of the infinite me and the other is all on the side of the finite me. It should surprise no one that a secret and sometimes not-so-secret war goes on between my two worlds. Or that spirit sometimes sings and sometimes seethes in my blood. That the Word sometimes tolls like a funeral bell in my mind and sometimes does a ragtime jig. And how grateful I am to that Word that it verifies in every way the truth of me, the truth of my nature, and refuses to leave out one single facet of that truth! God's Word and Christ's Secret Agent in this world force me to see, to face, and to accept all the implications of being what I am—body and spirit fused in one human being.

And what are these implications? Precisely this—*either* I can and may sink to the lowest low of my fallen nature (which is not to sink to the beast but *below* the beast, for the opposite of the divine is not the bestial but the demonic), *or* I can and may rise to the heights of my other, my divine nature, my noble birthright, my created-in-the-image-of-God birthright. Furthermore, my task in life is never to lose sight of the difference between myself and God. I am a'shudder insofar as I am *unlike* him and a'glow insofar as I am *like* him.

Hence I have two big pockets in my spiritual apron. When I feel a'shudder insofar as I am unlike him, when I am no friend of myself, when I hate myself, and, of course, as a natural consequence, hate everyone else and the whole stinking mad world as well, or when I feel most deeply the disparity between my action and God's intention for me, my hand goes instinctively to my right pocket, and I pull out this comforting reminder to myself:

> *Beloved, we are God's children now; it does not yet appear what we shall be, but we know that when he appears we shall be like him, for we shall see him as he is.*

And I ascend and soar with John.

And when my mind is drugged with the fumes of ego, and my self-opinion is most swollen and exaggerated, when I feel that I'm OK and you're OK and we're all OK, I put my hand in my other pocket.

> *I do not understand my own actions. For I do not do what I want, but I do the very thing I hate. . . . Wretched man that I am! Who will deliver me from this body of death?*

And I descend with Paul into the abyss of self.

Out of that same pocket I pull another discomforting reminder, so reminiscent of Paul that I marvel, for it is in Saul Bellow's 20th-century novel *Henderson the Rain King*.

*Oh, my body, my body! Why have we never really got together as friends? I have loaded it with my vices, like a raft, like a barge. Oh, who shall deliver me from the body of this death?*

My pockets yield other reminders to help me keep my spiritual equilibrium. In my right pocket:

*Yet thou hast made him little less than God,*
*and dost crown him with glory and honor.*

*Law came in, to increase the trespass; but where sin increased, grace abounded all the more, so that, as sin reigned in death, grace also might reign through righteousness to eternal life through Jesus Christ our Lord.*

*If God is for us, who is against us?*

*The Lord is my light and my salvation;*
*whom shall I fear?*

And in my left pocket:

*We have all become like one who is unclean, and all our righteous deeds are like a polluted garment. We all fade like a leaf, and our iniquities, like the wind, take us away.*

*All we like sheep have gone astray;*
*we have turned every one to his own way.*

*For there is no distinction; since all have sinned*
*and fall short of the glory of God.*

*For the wages of sin is death.*

*It we say we have no sin, we deceive ourselves,*
*and the truth is not in us.*

Psalm 139 has a place in both my pockets! As do also these lines from William Blake:

*O man, how great, how little thou!*
*O man, slave of each moment, lord of eternity!*
*Man was made for joy and woe;*
*And when we this rightly know*
*Through the world we safely go.*
*Joy and woe are woven fine*
*A clothing for the Soul divine;*
*Under every grief and pine*
*Runs a joy with silken twine.*

But how pale and puny are all the reminders in my left pocket compared to David's anguished cry for mercy in Psalm 51!

*For I know my transgressions,*
*and my sin is ever before me.*
*Against thee, thee only, have I sinned,*
*and done that which is evil in thy sight.*

"Hey, now! Wait a minute!" someone may think upon reading this. "Are we back in the Dark Ages of Christianity again? I thought we were all through with that harping on sin and an angry God and all that!"

Quite true! We do indeed live in an enlightened age that is too sophisticated and scientific to believe in hell and too busy to think about sin. Or, rather, our age is busily reconciling people to their sins and not to their God. As for Jesus Christ, his broken body and blood is not on the modern menu. If he is there at all, it is as a kind of Big Brother who somehow has provided us with a maximum of security and a modicum of suffering. For which we say, "Thank you, thank you, sweet Jesus!"

Please note that the counterparts in my counter-pockets are not: belief and disbelief, angel and devil, agreement and alienation, hope and hopelessness, happiness and unhappiness, health and disease, leniency with self and harshness with self, truth and error, virtue and sin, innocence and guilt. Instead they are: awareness of my fallen nature and awareness of my divine nature.

When I am most deeply aware of my fallen nature I am not at all doubting and disbelieving, demonically possessed, in hopeless despair, tragically unhappy, morbidly diseased, flagrantly in error, or wallowing in sin and guilt. On the contrary, I am so far removed from the clutches of the Evil One that he must be grinding his teeth to the gums. I am closer to heaven and hope and truth and happiness and a sound and healthy mind and spirit than ever in my life. Indeed, thanks to my Christian faith, I feel quite cheerful about my cheerless view of me. And that is the wonder of it! That is the joyous and flippant wonder of the Christian doctrine of the Fall!

Is this a game, then? See-Saw, Margery Daw! Now she's up! Now she's down! The downer her down, the upper her up! Pinch me blue so that I can feel how good I feel when it's over. Know your sin, and you're in, IN, *IN!*

Or even the game of Felix Culpa. If I were pure, I would never know salvation! Even Paul was accused of playing that game, as he wrote to the Romans: "And why not do evil that good may come?—as some people slanderously charge us with saying."

Or is this a kind of psychological game—the "Who Am I?" game? Only instead of answering and analyzing silly, superficial questions about how you squeeze the tube of toothpaste or which shoe you put on first, you analyze your sins, go through the stinking worm bag of all your faults. It could be sort of fun—like picking open old scabs.

If looking into the chasm of my fallen nature, if looking at my sins face to face is a game, then Lent is a game. And if Lent is a game, then it actually is far too tediously long. Games have their own law of waning interest and waxing tedium. Lent should be pared down to—to two weeks, perhaps?

Robert Herrick, 17-century poet, wrote these striking lines in "To Keep a True Lent."

*Is this a Fast, to keep*
*the larder lean?*
*And clean*
*From fat of veals and sheep?*
*Is it to quit the dish*
*of flesh, yet still*
*To fill*
*The platter high with fish?*
*Is it to fast an hour,*
*Or ragg'd to go,*
*Or show*
*A down-cast look and sour?*
*No: 'tis a Fast to dole*
*Thy sheaf of wheat*
*And meat*
*With the hungry soul.*
*It is to fast from strife*

*And old debate,*
*And hate;*
*To circumcise thy life.*
*To show a heart grief-rent;*
*To starve thy sin,*
*Not bin;*
*And that's to keep thy Lent.*

Robert Herrick was moving the keeping of Lent in the right direction, away from mortifications of the flesh—fasting, hair shirts, pebbles in the shoes, burrs next to the skin, dour faces, and all that. But he stopped somewhat short of the true purpose of Lent, which is not to starve one's sin but to get rid of it. And then—*then* comes spiritual energy, spiritual activity, spiritual eloquence, all so strongly manifested in Paul, who felt the depth of his sin and the exaltation of getting rid of it as did no other prophet or apostle.

Spiritual energy, activity, and eloquence do not come from ecstasy but from a humbly grateful heart. Forgiveness of sins is what the gospel is all about. Forgiveness of sins is what Christ's death upon the cross is all about. The purpose of Lent is to arouse. To arouse the sense of sin. To arouse the sense of guilt for sin. To arouse the humble contrition for the guilt of sin that makes forgiveness possible. To arouse the sense of gratitude for the forgiveness of sins. To arouse or to motivate the works of love and the work for justice that one does out of gratitude for the forgiveness of one's sins.

To say it again—this time, backward: There is no motivation for works of love without a sense of gratitude, no sense of gratitude without forgiveness, no forgiveness without contrition, no contrition without a sense of guilt, no sense of guilt without a sense of sin.

In other words, a guilty suffering spirit is more open to grace than an apathetic or smug soul. Therefore, an age without a sense of sin, in which people are not even sorry for not being sorry for their sins, is in rather a serious predicament. Likewise an age with a Christianity so eager to forgive that it denies the need for forgiveness. For such an age, therefore, Lent can scarcely be too long!

"I have found only one religion that dares to go down with me into the depth of myself," wrote G. K. Chesterton. And it is true. No other religion dares to take me *down* to the new beginning. Hence Lent is not a tediously long brooding over sin. Lent is a journey that could be called an upward descent, but I prefer to call it a downward ascent. It ends before the cross, where we stand in the white light of a new beginning. So fresh and new, says Chesterton, waxing lyrical, "that one can be grey and gouty—but only five minutes old!" The spirit that shuns this downward ascent all its livelong days eventually ends up an aged fetus. There is an infinite difference between being brand-new and five minutes old and being an aged fetus!

# HORIZONTAL EVASIONS OF SELF-SEEING

2 But to go down deep, deep, and deeper still is a terrifying experience, whether one is descending into one's own subterranean being or into a pitch black unknown by a very tangible stairway. I know, for I have done both. In the summer of 1939, my husband and I, very young and very free, were cycling on a tandem on the back roads of Germany through towns and villages that scarcely ever saw tourists. On a Sunday morning, we

cycled into a quiet village which seemed as if it were still in the Middle Ages. It lay at the foot of a hill, and at the top was the old ruin of a castle. We pushed our bike up the steep and cobbled path, parked it against a crumbling stone wall, and explored the ruins. It was enough like other castle ruins to merit no further comment, but when we returned to the tandem, Howard spotted the door in the wall. True to his investigative nature, he had to find out what lay behind it. A stone stairway descended into pitch darkness.

"No," I said.

"Why not?" he said.

Even with my hand clutched firmly in the hand of a very confident and resolute man, that descent into the unknown was terrifying to me. We quickly lost the light of day and were stumbling from landing to landing in utter darkness.

"Let's go back! We might drop off into a pit, an old torture chamber, or a bottomless underground lake—!"

"I have a pack of matches."

Sliding our free hands along damp and dripping walls, we felt our way down in the pale light of one paper match after another.

"Let's go back before it's too late—if it isn't already!"

"I have another pack of matches."

"Just *one?*"

"Just one."

"But we have to get back *up* again! And no one in the whole world knows that we're down here!"

"This has to end somewhere. I'm sure this was a secret passageway from the castle out beyond the walls to the open countryside."

Sure enough, when the last match flickered out we saw a squint, a square of daylight ahead. I now know precisely how Tom Sawyer and Becky felt when they saw the crack of light and the secret exit from the cave in which they had been lost for three days. Howard was right. That quarter mile of winding, descending stairway did lead beyond the castle and town walls into the open countryside. However! The exit through which that blessed light was coming was covered with an iron grating embedded in concrete!

Obviously we found our way back and lived to tell the story. I tell this tale merely to illustrate that descents into the unknown are terrifying, and it is no wonder that many persons consciously or unconsciously shun them and steer their lives away from them. And drop the a'shudder dimension out of their lives. And think Lent too long.

There are horizontal and vertical ways of avoiding the downward ascent. Of the horizontal evasions it is more painful and distressful for me to discuss the elusions and illusions of the brought-up Christians than of the "happy pagans," and it should not be at all hard to guess why—it is too close to home for comfort! Yet I am sure God's Secret Agent of Reform in this world finds no one quite so ungettable as good brought-up Christians whose good has gone wrong and they do not know it. When he makes his weekly report on them he no doubt shakes his head and says, "I've tried everything! Stung their souls with gadflies, scattered thorns in them—they simply tidy up their souls and go on thinking that spiritual stagnation is identical with the peace that passes all understanding. So cozy! So comfortable! Plain sailing! No mystery! Far from being haunted by the truth of themselves and of the cross, they bask in their virtues, idolize the cross, and loll in its shadow."

The twice-borners must give him trouble, too. When he makes his weekly report on them, he no doubt sighs and says, "There's no converting the converted. They stop at two, think that's enough, and don't seem to realize that a conversion is obsolete every day and that one can never be reborn enough."

Neither radiant saints nor flagrant sinners, many brought-up Christians drift along horizontally, never recognizing their true natures, never discovering their sins, and never being surprised by grace. Meeting their own standards of goodness and morality, tucked up in their cozy oversimplifications, they talk as if the Christian community, the Christian congregation, the Christian family, the Christian individual—really and truly Christian, that is—have no problems whatsoever with evil and suffering in the world or with evil and suffering within themselves. As if they themselves, being Christian, never felt the pangs of loneliness, confusion, doubt, anguish of mind or spirit. As if to admit that they had these feelings occasionally were to admit that they were not true or twice-born Christians.

Christ himself knew sharp anguish of spirit and expressed it. In Gethsemane: "Father, if thou art willing, remove this cup from me." On the cross: "My God, my God, why hast thou forsaken me?" They who shun the descending ascent themselves would perhaps be reluctant to believe that he who was divine had to take it, too, and thereby opened himself and his spirit to the sacred energy he needed in his darkest hour.

Be they brought-up or born-again Christians, many find their own private, inside world to be more or less a good, decent place. It is the world outside that is dreadfully sinful. It is the world of "them" that is a scandal. Such Christians believe very firmly in hell and the devil and that human beings are full of hell and that the devil is gleefully doing his damndest to fill his hell with human beings. Their trouble is with the word *me,* with making the transition from *them* to *me,* from "Old Adam in them" to "Old Adam in me." If they catch a glimpse of the ancient enemy in children, they do not recognize him as their own first and last enemy. If they see a grandchild push another down the stairway screaming "I hate you! I hate you!" they feel the child is being very naughty and is not being brought up right. That this lovely little girl with the pink complexion harbors a dark inheritance is too horrifying a thought to think. So, after a grandmotherly lecture on not having such naughty, naughty feelings, they dismiss the thought that could become a thorn in the spirit, a thorn of ultimate blessing.

Brought-up and born-again Christians who shun the descending ascent are abstractly aware that there are large concerns and tragic needs in the world at large, "but let us pray a little, give a little, and hope a lot, and everything will turn out in the end. At least there will be some improvement!" They do not face up to the painful, inch-by-inch, ongoing struggle to bring justice to this world, to alleviate the sufferings brought about by injustice, to root out the causes of injustice.

Many who do face that struggle know all the time that ultimately they cannot root out the radical, perennial root of their own human nature, yet they never use that as an excuse for accepting the world as it is and doing nothing! Many brought-up or born-again Christians have no inkling of this painful contradiction, no inkling that the possibles of all evil are as close as their own blood and bone. Their prayers could be boiled down to: "Benevolent and easy-going Father of us all, be thy own dear, sweet self and grant that we may go on living a happy comfortable, harmless life as good, decent, fairly normal people. Jesus, sweet Jesus, thank you for making it all possible."

Cozy, smug, oversimplifying Christians who shun the descending ascent are the target of Flannery O'Connor's short novels and stories. This was her quarrel with Christians, at least the Christians she saw in her little world in rural Georgia. Perusing the terrain of their souls with X-ray eyes, she saw that beneath the top layer of sweet, decent goodness was the deep of sin—and that even that top layer of goodness was sin camouflaged as good. The self-revelation one experiences looking into the mirror of Flannery O'Connor's stories is shocking, sometimes scandalously so—but no more shocking and scandalous than the Christian religion and Jesus Christ our Savior! In an essay in *Religion and Modern Literature* on O'Connor's writing (p. 369), Robert Drake writes:

> *Miss O'Connor's major theme should come as no surprise to us. It is that the Christian religion is a very shocking, indeed a scandalous business . . . and that its Savior is an offense and a stumbling block, even a "bleeding stinking mad" grotesque to many. He "upsets the balance around here"; He "puts the bottom rail on top"; He makes the first last and the last first. In short, He revolutionizes the whole Creation and turns the*

*whole world upside down, to the scandal of those who believe that two plus two always equals four (and, with craft, possibly five) or those who believe that they don't need any outside help (a savior) because they're doing all right by themselves. And this Christ comes not lamb-like and meek, as a rule, but in terrifying glory, riding the whirlwind: He is more like Eliot's "Christ the tiger" than gentle Jesus meek and mild. There is nothing sweet or sentimental about Him, and He terrifies before He can bless.*

After reading this, do you begin to suspect as I have long suspected—that it will not be the theologians but the great writers, or should we say *the great sighters,* who will take us back and set our feet firmly on ancient doctrines so that we may recover our lost heritage? We who have not abandoned these doctrines are sometimes shocked by these writers, but this was their explicit intention. As Flannery O'Connor herself said in an essay "The Fiction Writer and His Country": "To the hard of hearing you shout, and for the almost blind you draw large and startling figures." Or, to quote the late Spanish philosopher Unamuno: "The greater part of my work has been to disquiet my neighbors, to stir up the sediments of their hearts, to sow anguish in them." Or, as Kafka wrote: "The books we need are the kind that act upon us like a misfortune, that make us suffer like the death of someone we love more than ourselves, that make us feel as if we were on the verge of suicide or lost in a forest remote from all human habitation. A book should serve as the axe for the frozen sea within us."

Sin, judgment, and redemption are by no means archaic and obsolete to the Christians living on the horizontal, but they steer clear of those "heavenly hurts" that a sober exploration of the implications these doctrines might bring. They would rather not live in the sometimes painful but always electric tension between humiliation and redemption. They would rather go straight ahead on the comfortable horizontal path they know so well, wanting neither up nor down nor the way up that goes down. Not that they would do away with Lent. Indeed not, for Lent, after all, is a pious tradition, and pious traditions are not to be tampered with.

Yet "the terror" (the terrifying sense of good gone wrong and suddenly knowing it) does at times strike these Christian evaders of the downward ascent, as Walker Percy with acid clarity points out in his novel *Love in the Ruins* (p. 14):

> *Next door is Geriatric Rehabilitation or "Gerry Rehab," a far-flung complex of pleasant low-lying white-roofed Daytona-type buildings. Here old folks from Tampa to Tucson are treated for the blues and boredoms of old age. There good folks, whose physical ailments are mostly cured nowadays, who at 85, 90, even at 100, are as spry as can be, limber-jointed, smooth-faced, supple of artery, nevertheless often grow inexplicably sad. Though they may live in the pleasantest Senior Settlements where every need is filled, every recreation provided, every sort of hobby encouraged, nevertheless many grow despondent in their happiness, sit slick and empty-eyed at shuffleboard and ceramic oven. Fishing poles fall from tanned and healthy hands. Golf clubs rust.* Reader's Digests *go unread. Many old folks pine away and even die from unknown causes like victims of a voodoo cure. Here in Gerry Rehab, these sad old-*

> *sters are encouraged to develop their "creative and altruistic potential." Yet mysterious deaths, and suicides too, continue to mount. The last Surgeon General's report named the nation's number-one killer as "Senior Citizens' Anomie," known locally as the St. Petersburg blues.*

In Walker Percy's Florida retirement village, the brought-up and born-again Christians live side by side with the "happy pagans."

> *The scientists, who are mostly liberals and unbelievers, and the businessmen, who are mostly conservative and Christian, live side by side in Paradise Estates, though the two make much of their differences—one speaking of "outworn dogmas and creeds," the others of "atheism and immorality," etc. etc. To tell the truth, I do not notice a great deal of difference between the two. . . . On Sundays Christian businessmen dress up and take their families to church, whereas unbelieving scientists are apt to put on their worst clothes and go bird-watching. As one of my behaviorist friends put it, "My cathedral is the blue sky and my pilgrimage is for the ivory-billed woodpecker"* (p. 15).

This brings us to the horizontal evasions of those who consider the whole idea of the fallen nature of humanity, the moral burden of the individual, and the atonement on the cross to be inventions of the theologians. Failing to see the human predicament, failing to see themselves as human beings bearing within themselves a fallen nature at war with the divine in them, they do not perceive any need at all of standing before the altar of the broken body and blood of a savior. Indeed, the whole idea is repugnant to them. They escape—or attempt to escape—their own selves according to their own natural inclinations, but their slopes and tilts are never downward into themselves. Like Walker Percy's behaviorist, whose cathedral is the blue sky and whose pilgrimage is for the ivory-billed woodpecker, some of them escape into nature. Disdaining the dismal companionship of people who brood over their sins, they cheerfully turn to cheerful and cheering nature, which wastes no time or energy on such a fruitless or needless pastime.

But those who try to escape their human selves in nature eventually discover that they cannot be happy animals any more than they can become angels, for they are still human beings trapped in their human nature. This sad and progressive revelation of the inadequacy of nature is graphically recorded in the notebooks and writings of a 19th-century British writer and lay-naturalist, Richard Jefferies:

> *I never go for a walk in the fields without seeing one thing at least, however small, to give me hope. The frond of a fern among dead leaves. I rarely go for a walk in town without seeing something to cause depression, almost despair.* [Reminiscent of William Blake, who while walking in London saw in almost every human face "marks of weakness, marks of woe."]

> *For they [the things of nature] were so much to me, I had come to feel that I was as much to them. The old, old error: I love the earth; therefore the earth loves me—I am her child—I am Man, the favoured of all creatures. I am the Centre, and all for me was made.*

> *Nature sets no value upon life, neither of the snail or of the human being.*
>
> *The earth is all in all to me, but I am nothing to the earth; it is bitter to know this before you are dead.*
>
> *I have been through nature, I am weary of nature, nothing there. . . . I hate nature. I turn my back on it.*

Strangely enough, during a long illness Richard Jefferies thought his way through to a kind of doctrine of Original Physical Ill Health, but there is no trace of a notion of Original Spiritual Ill Health.

Again, from his notebooks: "Where shall I go to escape life? Disease is everywhere. We carry life with us and its dangers." On this same theme he wrote in *The Story of My Heart:*

> *The truth is, we die through our ancestors; we are murdered by our ancestors. Their dead hands stretch forth from the tomb and drag us down to their mouldering bones. . . . This day those that die do not die in the sense of old age, they are slain. . . . The only things that have been stored up have been for our evil and destruction, diseases, and weaknesses crossed and cultivated and rendered almost part and parcel of our very bones.*

Nature brings no real comfort. Rather than proving an escape, it asks more uncomfortable questions than the mind of a thinking person can bear—notably, questions about the suffering of all life, creaturely and human, but chiefly about the sufferings of children, for they are so helpless and innocent. It becomes necessary, then, to kill the God of nature—who, if he existed, ought to be ashamed of himself for letting there be so much misery in the world. Perhaps the saddest and most poignant comment I have read to that effect was made by Richard Jefferies. On seeing the misery of the children of the destitute, he jotted down in his notebooks: "If their God got up in the night they would not be pale, stunted, and wretched for life."

But killing God is an act of despair and does not solve the human problem, nor can nature solve or save. What do the everlasting hills care about people? And can a lovely lily bursting white save us—from ourselves? The God who can and does save people wrote only a faint signature in nature. On the cross, however, God wrote it in the red-red of blood—God's own blood.

# 3 VERTICAL EVASIONS OF SELF-SEEING

Vertical evasions of self-seeing are many, and as varied as they are many—but they can all be placed under the umbrella of The Big Search. For mystical union. For beatitude. For paradise on earth. For instant sainthood.

Is it because once upon an Adam-time we were ousted from paradise and always want to get back? And we always seek to get back by the path that soars? Christ without tears? Beatitude without sweat? New birth without labor cramps? Salvation without spiritual tribulation?

The Big Search for Mystical Union is more or less the enterprise of young people who have discovered that the world is tougher and that life is more complicated than they had imagined it to be. The cheese on the moon has turned out to be full of maggots. The yeast of their young exuberance has soured. "Ah, life, I would have been so pliant a thing / If you had left my little joys alone," wrote Edna St. Vincent Millay, the poet of youthful disillusionment. Kierkegaard, not such a poet but an expert diagnostician of the psyche, had one of his pseudonyms describe this spiritual malaise with the special skill and knowledge of one who has had the disease himself:

> *My life is utterly hopeless. I am nauseated by existence. It is insipid—without salt and meaning. Were I starving even more than Pierrot, I would not choose to eat the explanation people offer. One sticks a finger into the ground to smell what country he is in. I stick my finger into existence—it has no smell. Where am I? What does it mean—the world? What is the meaning of the word? Who tricked me into this situation and leaves me standing here? Who am I? How did I get here? Why wasn't I asked about it? . . . How did I get involved in this big enterprise called actuality? Why should I be involved? Isn't it a matter of choice? Am I compelled to be involved? Where is the manager—I have something to say about this. Is there no chairman? To whom shall I make my complaint?*

But long, long before either Millay or Kierkegaard—and far better than they—an ancient writer described this malaise of the spirit. Read, if you will, the Book of Ecclesiastes!

They wish and they want, they long and they hanker—these young people. For Experience. For Religious Experience. For Extraordinary Religious Experience. An Extraordinary Religious Experience which will put all their pieces together into one beautiful holy whole, and they will live in beautiful spiritual communion with other holified children of the light. Spontaneous, creative, authentic children, stripped of all the dross of technology and materialism. Simple wants. Simple joys. Free of all the clutter and clichés of institutional religions. Happy to be emancipated from "that former time when Love, Sweet Love, was thought a crime."

The Christian God is too much of an old parent, too establishment, to provide what they want. Moreover, their early pleas for all their wants had gone unanswered—as if God had moved away and their requests were placed in a dead-letter file. And so now they are listening and waiting and attending to any and every unqualified something or someone that will bring them what they want—escape from their sweating selves, from a dull and ordinary life, and from a rotten, rancid world. Like sheep bleating in any and every pasture, looking for a shepherd, they go seeking in Oriental religions, in transcendental meditation, in any cult or clique that promises a mystical union with something or other. Whether the Nirvana they find is reached by four noble truths or forty, by an eightfold or an eightyfold noble path, it is a moving from one state of nothingness to another, and the best response I know to it was made by an atheist (Cioran, *The Temptation to Exist):* "The

Israelites would have stoned Moses if he had addressed them in the language of a Buddha, the language of metaphysical lassitude, offering annihilation and salvation."

The Big Search in the new but ever-so-old religion of "doing my thing" is for self-identity, and the key words are "being an authentic person, being an individual, being creative, spontaneous. . . ." The frightening thing about this new relapse into ancient barbarism is that "doing my thing" is presented to youth as being the thing God wants them to do.

It is true that God wants me to have the identity given specifically to me and to no other. He wants me to be authentic, creative, spontaneous. But God is God, and in infinite wisdom God knows that one does not get that way by putting self in the center of one's life. Putting self in the center and making a religion of seeking self-satisfaction—creativity for the sake of self, spontaneity for the sake of self—brings one down, down, down into the crudest infantilism, the most excessive self-indulgence, and the most tragic self-delusion.

The Big Search for Beatitude is not restricted to women only, but it is most often their peculiar warp. Could it be that women seek to transcend the ordinary because they feel so very trapped in it? Do they crave the bless of bliss because their ordinary everyday lives seem so unblessed by it? Do they embrace a religion that promises beautiful feelings because the promise of them seems so absent from their lives?

Christianity impresses them with its promise of the fruits of the Spirit: love, joy, peace, patience, kindness, goodness, faithfulness, gentleness, self-control. All of these undeniably most beautiful fruits they mistakenly regard as beautiful feelings. They interpret the promise to mean that to live in the Spirit is forevermore to feel joyful, peaceful, patient, kind, good, faithful, gentle, and self-controlled. In other words, forevermore they will have positive feelings. Christianity becomes for them the religion of beautiful feelings, and they become the ready market for the purveyors of saccharine "Christian" art, cloying "Christian" music, uplifting "Christian" magazines and books. They become the faithful unseen audience for "soul-stirring" radio and TV programs. It is women who predominate in audiences at religious meetings that deliberately and with shrewd knowledge of the affective elements in the human psyche effect an emotionalism that can only be distrusted.

Kingdom Come does not come by the way of sensations, even uplifting ones. So-called mountaintop experiences are beautiful while they last, but they never do. And when they do not, women are smitten with guilt and a brand-new and negative feeling in addition to all the old negative ones—the feeling that if they are unable to have continuous and sustained beatitude then they are not Christian enough. They have failed again. They are once again back in sickly, morbid self-loathing—the ugliest of ugly feelings. They wait for the next uplifting experience culminating in the next feeling of beatitude. They read their Bibles "more religiously"—and this is the rub, for the Bible was never meant to be read religiously. They pray more feelingfully, but the essence of their prayers is that in their sensuous minds they might *feel* the beautiful feelings they feel that they ought to feel.

Becoming the new creation in Christ does indeed mean

that the fullness of life in him enters into the very tissue of our existence, but the fallenness of life is still present there as well. It has not been banished in any magical way. The fallen nature is forgiven. We are freed of its dominion, released from its sentence to death. But as long as our spirits are tenanted in our mortal frames, the fallenness of the mortal self is our shadow. In other words, my chief enemy is still myself, my "I," and I can still be the prey to human feelings that are anything but beautiful—anger, indignation, vexation, frustration, and all their variations and combinations—suffering feelings caused by the ongoing struggle between flesh and spirit in the battleground of my fleshly self. The Spanish poet-philosopher Unamuno was quite right when he said, "Only what is dead, inhuman, does not suffer."

The apostle of the downward ascent says it repeatedly when he speaks of the fruit of the Spirit as a humble and a contrite heart (not a head proudful of its beautiful feelings!). Read the Letter to the Philippians:

> *Do nothing from selfishness or conceit, but in humility count others better than yourselves. Have this mind among yourselves, which is yours in Christ Jesus, who, though he was in the form of God, did not count equality with God a thing to be grasped, but emptied himself, taking the form of a servant, being born in the likeness of men. And being found in human form he humbled himself and became obedient unto death, even death on a cross.*

> *Therefore . . . work out your own salvation with fear and trembling; for God is at work in you, both to will and to work for his good pleasure.*

*For it has been granted to you that for the sake of Christ you should not only believe in him but also suffer for his sake, engaged in the same conflict which you saw and now hear to be mine.*

No, the fruit of the Spirit is not canned and preserved in gleaming jars and set on mental shelves for the mind to look at and derive beautiful feelings from the looking. "My patience was once such a forlorn fruit, but just look at this year's crop!" "The jars on my kindness shelf are almost bursting their covers!" Love, joy, peace, patience, kindness, etc. are not feelings in the mind. They are the activity of the broken and contrite spirit that has taken the downward ascent and risen in the exuberance of forgiveness to work relentlessly and steadfastly the works of righteousness to the glory and praise of God. If Paul and Unamuno are right, then perhaps we ought to be more concerned over having nothing but beautiful feelings than be concerned over a deficiency or absence of them!

Of the poets alive and writing in the English language today, none has more boldly rejected sense-drugged religiousness (be it drugged by nature worship or dreams of mystical union or cravings for beatitude), none has more boldly proclaimed Christian dualism than Jack Clemo, a British poet virtually unknown in the United States. Clemo has not been educated beyond his village school in Cornwall and has not wandered from the clay pits of that village. At an early age he became deaf, and at the age of 40 he became blind, but with his inner ear and inner eye he sees and hears with Pentecostal clarity. He does not need the exquisites of flowers and stars and streams to sing, or stained glass windows and candles and organ tones to worship. He sings of the dry bare bones of dogma as other poets sing of spring and birch trees in bud. He sees the symbol of the cross in an excavator! "Yes, this is Christian art."

Here are two of his sparse poems, which reveal how a soul purged of all the pampering accoutrements of esthetics may have a healthier vision of faith, show how the cross "may bend closer to the neon lights than to the mystic's grotto."

*Sufficiency*

*Yes, I might well grow tired*
*Of slighting flowers all day long,*
*Of making my song*
*Of the mud in the kiln, of the wired*
*Poles on the clay-dump; but where*
*Should I find my personal pulse of prayer*
*If I turned from the broken, scarred*
*And unkempt land, the hard*
*Contours of dogma, colourless hills?*
*Is there a flower that thrills*
*Like frayed rope? Is there grass*
*That cools like gravel, and are there streams*
*Which murmur as clay-silt does that Christ redeems?*
*I have not heard of any, so I trace*
*The writings on bruised iron and purged clay face:*
*"Young son of man, be strong,*
*For as My dower is, so shall be your song.*
*There is no weariness for you,*
*For I will let you view*
*In a human flower the soft warm growth:*
*Her tidal sap has touched the soil of both*
*The real worlds that you scan,*

*And thus shall make you man.*
*In the heights you shall hymn but Godhead grim and*
*grey;*
*In the depths you shall hymn but clay."*

### Lunar Pentecost
(To Renée Martz)

*Scarred stillness of the brooding bone*
*In the slow wash of lunar light:*
*Such was my ghostly kingdom, a dreamer's land*
*Which the real heaven had to smite.*
*It smote with song—just a fire-flake*
*That clove a crater in my clay:*
*God's jazz-drums seemed to thunder*
*Where His lava broke away.*

*There's a roar in the lunar valley—*
*No blast with hard rock thudding down:*
*This is faith's new vein, a molten joy*
*Stinging the brooder's frown.*

*Grim ritual of the isolate self*
*Is doomed now, for the flame laps on:*
*The beating jazz-fire mounts the white skull,*
*Enfolds the credal skeleton.*

*Hot ragtime stains the austere track,*
*Bubbles and burns among my glacial clues;*
*I shall not find the way back*
*To the crag's lip and the wintry bruise.*

*A fire-flake has pierced my silence,*
*And a tongue responds—too deep*
*To be greyly solemn, too sure*
*Of heaven's glowing heart to let me sleep*

*With the sufferer's image, that cold fang*
*Of lunar mystery. Now I feel*
*God's gay eruption is bedrock truth*
*Our stoic solitudes conceal.*

Are we to disparage nature, then? Banish art, music, altars, candles, and everything that enhances and enriches our lives? Are we back to that grim formula: "If it makes you feel good, it must be sin"? By the immortal Bach, no! However, the inebriate soul may not be the soul visited by Spirit, but only the soul self-intoxicated by moods and feelings. Spiritual sobriety may be a better ground in which to grow the truest fruit of the Spirit—a broken and contrite heart. The downward ascent is a truer way to go up than to go straight up!

As a matter of fact, the greatest music, literature, and art have been produced by men and women who have ascended by the downward path. Bach's hot ragtime of the spirit was born in the sense of sin. "One of you shall betray me," speaks/sings the Christ in Bach's *St. Matthew's Passion,* and the recitative passes to the chorus of believers. "Is it I? Is it I? Is it I?" And then comes the impressive, full-toned cry of all humankind: "'Tis I, *my* sins betray Thee, who died to make me whole."

As for great literature, name one truly great book that does not have two radical roots—one, a profound self-knowledge where all illusions are shattered, the other, an absolute and ultimate confidence that transcends the merely physical self. So full of truths about you and me are the great books that they are documentaries of our own souls.

It is the same with great art. The essential impact of

seeing the self-portraits of Rembrandt, of Van Gogh, of Käthe Kollwitz, is the essential impact of discovering kinship. These artists have descended to the place of pain and faced their human condition, and it is *your* human condition, *my* human condition.

No, ultimately, there is no vertical escape in great music, literature, and art.

Pascal declared that it is dangerous to forget either one's greatness or one's smallness. The evaders of the downward ascent who try to create a paradise on earth are for the most part men—men with a colossal overconfidence in man. Either forgetting or ignoring the dualities of body/spirit, smallness/greatness, *or*, swinging radically to the "little less than God" concept of humanity, they have tried to establish a New Jerusalem here on earth. If they do not believe in God, they try to bribe us away from our sense of divinity by promising to establish a social and economic Utopia.

But whatever their shade of philosophy, be they free lovers, celibates, Rousseauian romanticists, idealists, transcendentalists, socialists, communists, spiritualists, pietists, adventists—the paradises on earth they attempt to create inevitably collapse. Their sweeter and loftier evaluation of huamanity goes bankrupt in humanity's fallenness. Whatever happens at the end of their bright new departures, the end always confirms some born-with flaw in human nature.

No one has confessed this more candidly than did Upton Sinclair, whose ideal community, Helican Hall, organized in 1906, lasted but six months. He humorously reported parent conflicts sparked by incidents as simple as a mix-up of children's toothbrushes. (The children, incidentally, decided what was right and wrong for them in a Children's Parliament. Sinclair reports of a three-year-old popping up and saying, "All in favor say Aye!") "We learned more about human nature than we ever thought existed," he wrote. Even those who had had the best opportunities, he reported, turned out to be "utterly human when their thin veneer of 'civilization,' 'idealism,' 'altruism,' was penetrated."

Is this to say that Christian community or a Christian community is impossible? If somehow the Christian view of humanity has become unchristian and is infiltrated by the heresy of human perfectibility—yes, then a Christian community is impossible. But Christian communities built upon the sound and healthy Christian view of humanity as a duality not only are possible but do exist. They exist because they are not trying to be paradises on earth. Having no swollen self-estimates that need to be punctured, Christians living communally have a saving sense of humor because they are saved, know from what and for what they are saved, and know that they need to be saved every day. When visiting church women being shown a Catholic Worker Community in the ghetto of a large city paled at the smells and panicked at a cockroach scuttling across the communal kitchen, their priest guide quietly said, "Ladies, we do not have a single cockroach here. They are all married and have large families."

A saving sense of humor is precisely what perfectionist men and women trying to create a Utopia of their families do not have. How can they if they feel that they have been saved to make a perfect model of a Christian family? Bernanos describes a perfectionist woman in *The*

*Diary of a Country Priest*. She was the priest's vestry woman, and her goal

> *wasn't to fight dirt but to do away with it altogether, as if that were possible! A parish is bound to be dirty. A whole Christian society's a lot dirtier. She wasn't a real housewife; a real housewife knows her home isn't a shrine. Those are just poet's dreams.*

Like this vestry-cleaning woman, the perfectionist would sweep God himself out of the family in order to make a clean, respectable place of it. In their zeal for perfection, women have perhaps created more pain, frustration, and suffering in the family than any other member—unless it is the perfectionist father. The suffering of living under a perfectionist father is devastatingly described in Kafka's *Letter to His Father*.

> *I was continually in disgrace; either I obeyed your orders, and that was a disgrace, for they applied, after all, only to me; or I was defiant, and that was a disgrace too, for how could I presume to defy you; or I could not obey because I did not, for instance, have your strength, your appetite, your skill, although you expected it of me as a matter of course; this was the greatest disgrace of all.*

Nathaniel Hawthorne and Herman Melville each wrote a thundering "No!" to the heresy of human perfectibility. In a story heavy with symbolism, Hawthorne wrote of a young husband who delighted in the flawless beauty of his bride's soul and in her almost flawless physical beauty. However, a tiny birthmark on her face gradually became to him the horrible symbol of the fatal flaw in human nature, a symbol of his wife's susceptibility to sin and death. He resorted to magic and sorcery to remove this flaw and in the process destroyed both his wife and himself.

Hawthorne suggests that in a desperate attempt to make a flawed and imperfect world perfect, we make it more flawed and imperfect—and sometimes demonically so. In the name of making a more perfect world, perfectionists will kill anybody who gets in their way, will destroy whole populations, all those whose flaws and defects keep their world imperfect.

Is it Yes to imperfection and No to perfection, then? Yes to impiety, No to piety? Yes to evil-doers, No to do-gooders? Yes to self-indulgence, No to abstinence? Yes to reprobates, No to saints? Yes to sin, No to sanctification? Yes to the oldness of Old Adam, No to the newness in Christ?

The finger of the Holy Spirit has traced the call to be perfect, to be saints, to newness in Christ, on every page of the New Testament. It is written in blood on the cross. There is no evading that call! But thanks be to God, the communion of saints is not based on human perfectibility but assumes its imperfection and imperfectibility. Our God has chosen to become involved in the divine failure—humanity. Our Savior chose to share with us the pain, punishments, and penalties of being imperfect humans. And God's Secret Agent of Reform chooses to help us imperfect creatures respond to the terrible call to be new creatures in Christ. For it *is* a terrible call, and it is a long, long, painful journey. For there is so much to tear down before the Holy Spirit can build up. There are so many fake props to knock down. And the end of the painful road is not perfection, but perfect humility. Not morbidity and self-loathing, but a humble and contrite heart.

# DEAD-END DESCENTS

# 4

But even the downward path can take a wrong turn and end in an abyss of negatives, instead of ending in the flint-clean, rib-rock shaft where one dies to self and gets self back new, where

*When the vein is touched, the signal granted*
*Comes the sharp snap of blast*

*As the agnostic rock is splintered*
*and the barrier passed.*

JACK CLEMO
"Clay Phoenix"

Along the miss-taken path one comes instead to a place of gloom where those for whom God is dead sit on a heap of bat dung and wait for the end.

It is not guilt, not even false guilt, that drives some people into the depths of dead-end despair. If they are atheistic psychologists, then sin is nonsense and there is no such thing as guilt, there is only environmental conditioning. If they are atheistic communists, then sin is nonsense, the invention of capitalistic ecclesiastics who wish to keep people in fear and bondage. For them all negatives in life are the result of class struggle and economic injustice, and if there is any such thing as guilt it is class guilt. If they are atheistic intellectuals, then sin is nonsense. There is no such thing as guilt. There are only super-inflated human egos that do not know the human limitations and the absurdity of being human. "For those who feel, life is a tragedy; for those of us who think, life is a comedy."

Yes, at the end of one of these dead-end descents there is a theater of the absurd, where the intellectual elite sit in their boxes or up front in the parquet watching the absurd comedy of life. They have made the same decision that nonintellectual Stubb, a character in *Moby Dick,* made while standing alone on the deck on the midnight watch:

> *Ha, ha, ha! Clear my throat! —I've been thinking over it ever since, and that ha, ha's the final consequence.*

> *Why so? Because a laugh's the wisest, easiest answer to all that's queer; and come what will, one comfort's always left—that unfailing comfort is, it's all predestined. . . . I know not all that may be coming, but be what it will, I'll go to it laughing.*

Or, as Søren Kierkegaard has one of his pseudonyms say:

> *"Done for," they say, "We are done for! Nobody should complain about anybody—so let's all laugh. The crazier, the better," they say. "Let's not only be miserable scoundrels, but refine it with witty and clever knowledge and virtuosity in depicting it dramatically."*

There is also a library of modern literature and a gallery of modern art down in the depths of dead-end despair. Having abandoned the gospel of a God who cares and the myth of progress and enlightenment, the ha-ha mentality of this kind of drama, literature, and art raises its voice in one joint chorus: "The world is a mess, life is disgusting, but don't drown yourself in feelings. Just join us in the laughter."

For many thinking people, it is a deep sense of the colossal suffering in the world and not a deep sense of personal guilt that sends them into dead-end despair, and we who believe in Christ and in life as a divine comedy are not to sit in the Christian gallery in the theater of life, looking down on them and feeling ourselves saved and superior. We, the Christian elite, the happy few, we who are sorry for our sins, are not to look down on them, the intellectual elite and the miserable many who cannot even be sorry that they are not sorry, for they have no sins to make them sorry!

"Look at those godless pagans! Look at them squirm! Listen to them whine! Well, they have it coming! They killed God. They flushed morality and conscience down the toilet. Let them suffer for it!" It would be far better for us *to suffer with* those who say, "How can we believe in the existence of a good and loving God who is all-powerful and at the same time all-compassionate when there is so much pain and suffering in the world?" Far better for us to acknowledge the presence of pain and suffering in the world as "the atheistic fact," as the great obstacle to religious or to Christian faith.

Merely accepting the fact of all this suffering and sitting confidently and smugly in the family of God, taking our Christian faith for granted, may well be another atheistic fact! For the nonbeliever, our smug Christian complacency about all the suffering in the world is one added obstacle to religious or Christian faith. Indeed, God looking at the uninterrupted, no-intermission drama of life here on planet earth may well see no difference at all between the immorality of pagans and the immoral morality of self-righteous Christians.

It might benefit us Christians, especially the easy optimists among us, to take—just once!—that dead-end path of adding up the quantity of suffering in the world. Just once to feel the sum of all suffering as Josephine Johnson felt the sum of tent worms the year the tent worms invaded and devastated the countryside: "Every worm is 200 worms. 200 x 200=40,000. Forty thousand times forty thousand . . . a little multiplying brings despair." If we do take that path we are not in ignoble company but in the company of many noble souls, both factual and fictional. Job and Jeremiah of the Old Testament, for example. Ivan in Dostoyevsky's *The Brothers Karamazov*. Ishmael in *Moby Dick*. Yes, even Mark Twain, for under his scintillating wit and humor was a black despair over the riddle of human suffering.

Perhaps every one of us in the family of God should take that journey whenever we feel the gloat of superiority over those who have no God. But we must be sure that we take that journey with a round-trip ticket! We are not to collapse with them in despair or in the black laughter of despair. We are not, as Flannery O'Connor perceptively claims our age does, we are not to domesticate despair and learn to live with it happily. If we take the journey honestly and humbly—not as tourists but as fellow-sufferers—we may come to understand that many nonbelievers are grappling honestly with one of the toughest problems of the human spirit. We may come to understand the loneliness of those who flee from nothingness and yet go relentlessly forward toward the death that to them is nothingness. If we stand beside them in humble and sympathetic understanding, we may be able to help them—not with easy, pat answers, not by flinging Bible verses at them, but by the quiet assurance that the God they have abandoned surely has not abandoned them.

In the no-God's land we may even find saints—saints without God, just as in the family of God we find reprobate saints, forgiven sinners whose psyches will never shine. In his essay "A Free Man's Worship," Bertrand Russel has erected the scaffolding for a humane and compassionate life on what he himself calls "the firm foundation of unyielding despair." There is no God, he declares, life is despair, but be defiant in your despair. Be a man and do your best for man. Life is a long march through the night to a common doom, but defy your fate, march along with your fellow–doomed courageously, lightening each other's burdens along the way.

If they sing hymns in no-God's land, they no doubt sing one by Swinburne: "Glory to man in the highest, for he is the master of things." If they have a gospel it is: In the beginning was nothing, and in the end there will be nothing, and we must be satisfied with that. As for their compassion grounded on defiant despair, it, too, is under the silent sentence of death.

"By God, I *will* do good!"

"By God? But your God is dead."

"By Jupiter, then! Or by Jove!"

"But the pagan gods are long since dead."

"By humanity, then!"

"By humanity? By Caligula? By Messalina? By Delilah? By Judas? By Hitler? By every man or woman whose natural reason and decency and dignity have collapsed and in whom the ancient evil in humanity has come to reign supreme?"

It is easy to abandon a god created in the image of man, but for those who cannot conceive of themselves as bearing the image of God, it is also easy to abandon —humanity!

Perhaps the descending shaft into the despair of no-God should not be called dead-end, for it is endless, descending ever deeper. Søren Kierkegaard has plumbed its depths in *The Sickness unto Death* and *The Concept of Anxiety,* but he did not pretend to have penetrated that shaft to its innermost.

Shooting off in the labyrinth of despair, but in an opposite direction, is *the despair of God,* which in a way is also a kind of atheism, for it is the despair of those who know only an angry God and despair of his grace, of his forgiving love. Whether they be the victims of harsh preaching of the law or have themselves twisted grace into another kind of law, the result is the same. They have no peace of conscience. They torture themselves with self-accusations, and become addicted to dejection.

While despairers of no-God do good works to defy the meaningless of existence, the despairers of God do good works in terror and dread of a merciless deity who has the power to send them to hell and damnation. These are the infamous works of "work righteousness," upon which so much scorn has been heaped that they seem like works of the devil. Perhaps the devil's actual work is to strike such terror into human souls that they perceive God as a tyrant father who exacts work from his children by caning and cudgeling them.

Søren Kierkegaard has pretty well explored this shaft of the human soul, too, in *Works of Love.* In his novel *The Scarlet Letter,* Nathaniel Hawthorne has explored the unforgivingness, heartlessness, and cruelty created in the hearts of humans by this view of God. Clarence Day, author of *Life with Father,* describes the painful ambiguity created by not clearly knowing whether God is angry or forgiving. Clarence Day's God was like his own father, full of wrath and affection. Both fitfully came and went, and neither could be counted on. "If I could have been sure that the Creator was my ally, or friend," he wrote, "that would have been a great comfort in those days. It would not only have saved me from worry, it would have set me free to go about my business with confidence, both in Him and myself."

In his later years, Mark Twain's despair of God led him to look upon life as a colossal practical joke on the part of the supreme practical joker, God. Melville says in *Moby Dick:* "Small difficulties and worryings, prospects of sudden disaster, pine of life and limb; all these, and death itself, seem . . . jolly punches in the side bestowed by the unseen and unaccountable old joker." Josephine Johnson writes in *The Inland Island:* "I think it is disgusting/ To praise God/ For making us acknowledge His presence/ By a poke in the eyeballs/ With his sharp stick."

But now we are veering back to the despair of no-God. How close the two are, after all—the despair of no-God and the despair of God!

A painful descending path that may end at the bottom and never ascend is the path of false guilt. There are three kinds: (1) The false guilt of being a brought-up or born-again Christian and yet not being as perfect as you think a brought-up or born-again Christian ought to be. In other words, the false guilt created by twisting grace into law. (2) The false guilt of having secret doubts about God and your Christian faith. (3) The false guilt for being angry with God, sometimes even hating him.

Christian grace twisted into law makes life a disease, for one is dis-eased by living in a feeling of continual disgrace. Well-meaning Christians are often guilty—and this is *real,* not false guilt!—of laying upon others the burden of a new law, a law requiring them to prove to the world their instant sanctification, their instant sainthood. As if sanctification were not a lifelong process! As if our imperfect and difficult personal and private psyches did not stay with us to the last breath of mortal life!

A Christian carpenter working one day in a Carthusian monastery was profoundly shocked when the monks, pledged to silence, suddenly rose up from their noon luncheon tables and began throwing and breaking dishes to express their pent-up rage over the daily inedibles the cook was serving them.

Many a Christian mother often feels like an anti-mother, an anti-woman, a monster, when she catches herself resenting her children's constant demands upon her. She is driven to despair by her own feelings and thinks that she has failed her children and failed her God. Indeed, she thinks she cannot possibly be a Christian, a true Christian, for a Christian mother would, of course, always be tender, loving, patient, etc. and would always feel blessed by her role as mother.

When there is death in a family, some Christians feel a false guilt for their very real grief and public display of it. Are they not betraying Christ, who won the victory over death? "O death, where is thy sting; O grave, where is thy victory?" But the death of their beloved *does*, nevertheless, sting, and their hearts are breaking!

But did not Christ himself openly and publicly grieve upon the death of his good friend Lazarus? Was he not openly and publicly angered by people's rejection of the kingdom? Was he not hurt by Judas's betrayal? And in his final agony, did he not cry out against God?

Having emotions is a part of being human, and a fully human person is bound to have a rich and wide diversity of them. Rather than waste feelings of guilt on feelings and temptations that may not be nice and respectable but are normal, perhaps we should thank God that we are manifestly human! The crucial point is not in having human feelings and human temptations, but in not letting them rule over us.

President Carter raised many a Christian eyebrow, as well as cynical secular eyebrows, when he confessed to little lusts.

If and when a little lust sneaks into the mind, rather than torture oneself with guilt over having it, there may be greater victory in saying, "Aha! There you are, you little lust! No, don't duck and hide! Come on out in the open and let me look you in the face! You are friend as well as foe, you know! You prove that I am not physically and sexually dead. Come, now, don't hide! I have another power, as well—my spirit! It needs exercise and may just as well get exercise in fighting *you!* I have an ally, as well—rather a formidable Power—and if you are as unholy as he is holy, then you had better watch out! Come here and let's see you face him!"

Not that there is not a real and terrible guilt and a real and terrible suffering associated with sex, love, marriage, and family. There is no pain in life equal to that which two lovers, husband and wife, parent and child, can inflict upon each other. It is when we hurt those whom we love most that our guilt becomes intolerable. That specific guilt and suffering is perhaps more intense in today's generation, when society no longer seems to elevate marriage, parenthood, and family life and seems merely to be waiting for the next titillating news of who is sleeping with whom.

It is perhaps more necessary now than at any previous time to understand the guilts and sufferings of young people caught in the middle in a revolution that is either moving us toward a new era of a deeper and more true union between man and woman and a new and more true reality of family life—or toward a jungle life of promiscuity where the constant changing of bed companions is normal, "provided there is love," as they say! This confusion and guilt are a real suffering that has to be faced and suffered through, and it is not simply a matter of banning erotic literature and pornographic films!

It is also a dead-end path and a waste of time and feelings to worry and feel guilty about spiritual doubts. Here, again, it would be more efficacious to invite the sneaking doubt out into the open arena of the mind and wrestle with it as Jacob wrestled with the Stranger. Indeed, doubt may be the Stranger encountering us, arousing us from the sleep of habit, challenging us to ask Jacob's question, "Tell me, I pray you, your name." In my own life and experience I have come to see that periods of doubt and "dry" periods are times of testing and trying that God in the mystery of divine purpose allows me to have. When I have felt God most absent he proves to have been most present—perhaps to teach me once again that faith is not a matter of feelings!

It is likewise a dead-end path and a waste of time and feelings to feel guilty about occasionally being angry with God, about crying, "How dare you, God!" Or, when one feels intensely the weight of universal suffering or one's own personal suffering, crying "Why, oh why?" If God is truly the Parent we believe him to be, then I am sure he esteems a quick and angry "Why do you have to strike so hard!" more highly than a "Thank you, thank you, Daddy, dear Daddy for spanking me! I know it is for my own good and that I richly deserve it!" God would, I suspect, perceive the angry, scolding response as proof of a closer and more intimate relationship than the instant raising of praise.

One of the many aspects of the Old Testament I especially love is the devout Jew's relationship to God. To the Jew, God was not distant, a God whose door you never expect to be opened no matter how hard you bang upon it, or a God who expected only honeyed phrases and sweet praises. To this day devout Jews (as in *Fiddler on the Roof)* speak to their Lord in a way that leaves no doubt that they expect a response, even if it is to have God suddenly open the door and roar "No!" What is the Book of Job but a scolding poem—Job scolding God and God scolding Job, Job hurling questions at God out of the aching, anguished cage of his finite self, and an infinite, personal God thundering a reply?

No, it is not spiritual arrogance to ask God an angry or an anguished *Why?* It is rather a proof of an intimate relationship with God and of an openness to God's answer. Every tribe and every nation that has believed in something "out there" has hurled this full-blooded, full-throated *Why?* at the throne of omnipotence itself. Not a weak whining and whimpering, but a lusty *Why?* that turns impossibility into possibility.

All of which brings us, finally, to the path of real guilt, by which we do not descend to sit and stew in morbid feelings of failure and false guilt, but by which we descend to the despair of self in which the impossible becomes possible. It is the gutsy guilt and despair of self that cries out with David:

*Have mercy on me, O God,*
*according to thy steadfast love;*
*according to thy abundant mercy*
*blot out my transgressions.*
*Wash me thoroughly from my iniquity,*
*and cleanse me from my sin!*

*For I know my transgressions,*
*and my sin is ever before me.*
*Against thee, thee only, have I sinned,*
*and done that which is evil in thy sight,*
*so that thou art justified in thy sentence*
*and blameless in thy judgment.*

# THE SELF AT THE FOOT OF THE CROSS

# 5

"Oh, my body! My body!" groans Henderson in Saul Bellow's *Henderson the Rain King*. "Why have we never really got together as friends? I have loaded it with my vices, like a raft, like a barge. Ah, who shall deliver me from the body of this death? Anyway, from these distortions owing to my scale and the work performed by my psyche. And sometimes a voice has counseled me crazily, 'Scorch the earth. Why should a good man die?

Let it be some blasted fool who is dumped in the grave.' What wickedness! What perversity! Alas, what things go on within a person!"

"Did you ever look inside yourself and see what you are not?" the crippled daughter in one of Flannery O'Connor's short stories shouts at her spiritually crippled mother. Few of us have looked long enough into ourselves to see that what seems to us and to others as normally attractive is actually as graceless as a scarecrow and even repulsive. It is an easy matter for the physical eye to spot physical deformity and blemishes in others and in oneself. It is not so easy for the eye of the spirit to spot a spiritual dwarf, hunchback, or cripple, although it is easier to see these spiritual deformities in others than in oneself. It is easier to see the is-ness and the is-not-ness and the ought-ness of another than to see one's own.

This X-ray look at others is called "naked truth," "unvarnished truth." In literature and art it is called realism. But to spot it in one's self is not only difficult but painful, and no one wants to take the descending path to that naked, unvarnished truth, with all its unacceptable humiliations. It is much more comfortable to stay on the level of the plain and ordinary, to go on being just plain and ordinary. Yet it is to this path that Lent invites us. The reason Lent is so long is that this path to the truth of oneself is long and snagged with thorns, and at the very end one stands alone before the broken body crowned with thorns upon the cross. All alone—with not one illusion or self-delusion to prop one up. Yet not alone, for the Spirit of Holiness, who is also the Spirit of Helpfulness, is beside you and me. Indeed, the Spirit of Helpfulness has helped to maneuver you and me down that dark, steep path to this crucial spot.

"But I've been to that place before," the born-again Christian may protest. "Of course, the non-Christian and perhaps the brought-up Christian need to be brought to that crucial spot, but of all people, we who are born again should not. Is it not a kind of heresy to say that we need to go there again and again and again? Is it not to doubt our salvation, the power of our Savior to deliver us from the dominion of darkness?"

Lent would indeed be a futile liturgical farce if the redeemed were henceforth sinless and if the tides of human nature were not always moving even the twice-born, who have not shed their human nature, in the direction of complacency and taking it all for granted. The tides of God always move in exactly the opposite direction—toward an ever deeper scepticism about ourselves (that we may have all the more confidence in God), toward an ever deeper self-distrust (that we may trust in God all the more). The high tides of human nature, even of the twice-born, move to drown the conscience. As long as the consciences of the born-again are housed in human flesh and bone, they are prone to the sleep of death and need continual rescuing.

Our self-indulgent and self-flattering age looks upon the self-maltreating and self-hating practices of the monastic and desert ascetics as pathetic and futile. We shiver to think of Suso making himself a cross with 30 protruding nails and wearing it on his back like a porcupine skin day and night. We laugh to think of him never taking a bath in order to mortify his comfort-seeking body. But for us who feel the need for daily showers (because soap has not broken dirt's dominion), it most certainly is not spiritual self-mortification and asceticism that convince us we no longer need spiritual shower baths. It is rather our comfort-seeking spirits.

But the spirit of truth does not seek comfort. And the born-again Christian needs the bath of self-severity as much as the brought-up and the un-Christian. The purpose of Lent is not to escape the conscience, but to create a hearty hatred for evil, a heartfelt contrition for sin, and a passionately felt need for grace. This continuous movement of faith from a sense of sin to grace and forgiveness ends only when spirit is ultimately released. This is splendidly expressed in John Donne's "Hymn to God the Father":

*Wilt Thou forgive that sin where I begun*
*Which is my sin, though it were done before?*
*Wilt Thou forgive those sins through which I run,*
*And do them still, though still I do deplore?*
*When Thou hast done, Thou hast not done,*
*For I have more.*

*Wilt Thou forgive that sin by which I won*
*Others to sin and made my sin their door?*
*Wilt Thou forgive that sin which I did shun*
*A year or two, but wallowed in a score?*
*When Thou hast done, Thou hast not done,*
*For I have more.*

"The sickness of our age is the failure of conscience rather than the failure of nerve," wrote Abraham Joshua Heschel. What a dull and static thing is a faith without a conscience! Or a faith where conscience is declared to be obsolete because "Now I have attained."

The most eloquent expression of gratitude for conscience I have read is in *The Cruciality of the Cross* by that splendid British preacher and theologian, P.T. Forsyth (who, incidentally, read Søren Kierkegaard and injected healthy doses of his thought into the flabby fiber of late 19th-century liberal theology). I take the liberty of phrasing his praise as the lyrical hymn it actually is. I apologize to P.T. Forsyth for some minor deletions and alterations in punctuation.

*Hymn to the Conscience*

*There is in the soul a bar, a tribunal.*
*Our thoughts and actions are ranged*
*before it. Judgment is passed there*
*upon what we have been*
*upon what we have done.*

*Talk of public opinion!*
*What is it in severity and power*
*to private opinion—*
*to a man's most private opinion*
*of himself?*

*We cannot get rid of this judge.*
*He is not in our power.*
*We cannot unmake him—*
*though he be against ourselves.*

*Then we did not make him!*
*He is an incorporate part*
*of our own being*
*our other self.*

*Wedded to us forever.*
*Wedded under laws that allow no divorce—*
*not for any incompatibility, cruelty, or infidelity.*

*What a strange thing we are!*
    *Two—*
    *yet one!*
*Two that cannot agree—*
*one that cannot be severed.*
*Our enemy is our essence,*
*taken from under our heart.*
*We are one by being two.*
*We are unhappy both because we are two*
    *and quarrel*
*and because we are one*
    *and cannot part.*

*Neither of us can go out of the other's*
*hearing. We may cease to attend much*
    *to each other*
*but we are always within call.*
*And every now and then—*
*in the depth of our neglect—*
    *we are called*
    *and we quail.*

*And it is then that some men curse*
*the voice they thought gone*
*and do the desperate things which*
*outsiders think so inexplicable.*

*Oh,*
*people did not know*
*what went on inside—*
*inside the spirit's house!*

Like Paul, who on occasion broke into poetry and lapsed again into prose, P.T. Forsyth also descended from rapturous statement to Saxon prose. Was it because this truth about conscience was so burning, so divine that he could not trust it to the quixotry of rapturous feelings?

> *Conscience is the Word of God within us; and moral responsibility means responsibility before God, the Living God, and Christ, His living Grace. Christ was and is the conscience of mankind and of God. He called Himself man's final judge. Was He deluded? He stands in the whole race as conscience does in each man. But He also means that the Eternal Conscience is the Eternal Love, that judgment is, in the heart of it, grace, that the judge is on our side, and is our Redeemer. It is only love that can do justice, it is only grace that can right all wrong. The righteous Lord whom we cannot escape is our Saviour.*

Still Forsyth—only the italics are mine: "*The conscience cries for forgiveness, and the Saviour of the conscience brings us to the Cross.*"

Here and here alone is the only escape from real guilt for sin (including the real guilt of having false guilts), and any thinking about, reflecting upon, or brooding about sin and guilt that does not end here is as futile as a carnival Lent. Here at the foot of the cross one raises *simultaneously*, as did Paul, the twin cries that belong together in the greatest of all paradoxes, demonstrating once again the upside-downness of the gospel and of a faith where the way up is the way down. "Wretched man that I am! Who will deliver me from this body of death?" wrote

Paul to the Romans, and in the very next line exclaimed, "Thanks be to God through Jesus Christ our Lord!"

But the twin cries are found in the Old Testament, as well. "Out of the depths I cry to thee, O Lord! Lord, hear my voice!" wrote David. And in another psalm: "God is our salvation. Our God is a God of salvation; and to God, the Lord, belongs escape from death." In a meditation on the twenty-third psalm, the late C.M. Granskou, formerly president of St. Olaf College, made this significant observation:

> *Its position in the Book of Psalms may be of no great significance and yet it suggests a thought to us. The twenty-second psalm is the psalm of the cross. It is the song of lamentation, of frustration and despair. The twenty-fourth psalm is the psalm of the crown, the song of triumph and victory and jubilation. Between these two great experiences of the human race, man's tribulations and his triumphs, his cross and his crown, there is the guiding hand of a loving God who cares and feels and knows.*

These twin cries are heard wherever there is a soundly Christian view of humanity. Even in music! At an organ concert in a Copenhagen church I heard the two cries in two separate organ chorales. It was "Ah, woe is me!" music, but in each of the chorales one of the variations broke away from the sad theme and *danced.* In Jack Clemo's poems, as well, I hear the "doggerel of Heaven," "God's foolishness" laughing through the gray, grim truth of me.

As for literature, if it does not contain the twin cries, it is not great literature. Much so-called Christian literature does not achieve greatness because it does not have the deep cry of humanity's suffering dilemma. As for modern writing, which so devastatingly depicts humanity at its worst, much of it cannot achieve greatness, because humanity's greatness is in the image of God, and this image has been murdered in modern fictional characters. Modern humanity, so lacking in magnificence, seems unable to cry: Holy, Holy, Holy, is the Lord of Hosts! As a matter of fact, modern humanity can scarcely cry at all—incapable of descent to humility as of ascent to magnificence—for if one cannot descend to a "Wretched man that I am!" he cannot rise to a "Thanks be to God through Jesus Christ our Lord!"

These twin cries confirm Abraham Heschel's statement that Christianity goes beyond Judaism on two points in its view of humanity—one more deeply pessimistic than any other religion, the other breathtaking in its optimism. They also confirm a healthy tension between the two seemingly opposing points of view in the Christian view of humanity: (1) the optimistic conviction that we are created in the image of God, created for Spirit, for the eternal, for eternity, and for life with God here and now and forever; (2) the pessimistic conviction of our infidelity, our traitorous infidelity to the living God, to the spirit within us, to the eternal within us.

There is a healthy tension between the pessimism of the doctrine of the Fall and the optimism of the staggering doctrine of Redemption. A healthy tension between the pessimistic conviction that our human plight is far worse than most of us realize and that our human possibility to live on a new plane of life is more amazing than we have let ourselves believe. A healthy tension between being serious about sin and being serious about salvation.

What happens down there at the foot of the path of real guilt, at the bottom of human despair of self, at the foot of the cross? The apostle writers call it a dying-to-self and a passing from death to life. Kierkegaard also called it dying to self, followed by the leap of faith in the Christ of the cross. And then? Kierkegaard is at a loss to describe the miracle. The pseudonymous author of *Fear and Trembling* writes:

> *The dialectic of faith is the most delicate and the most extraordinary of all; it has an elevation of which I can certainly form a conception, but no more than that. I can make the mighty trampoline leap whereby I cross over into infinity; my back is like a tightrope dancer's, twisted in my childhood, and therefore it is easy for me. One, two, three—I can walk upside down in existence, but I cannot make the next movement, for the miraculous I cannot do—I can only be amazed at it!*

Nobody has ever *explained* it and most attempts to do so wrong either God or humanity or both. It seems to be out of the realm of human enlightenment to go beyond Paul and what he quite simply says, as in the first chapter of his letter to the Colossians:

> *He has delivered us from the dominion of darkness and transferred us to the kingdom of his beloved Son, in whom we have redemption, the forgiveness of sins. . . . For in him all the fullness of God was pleased to dwell, and through him to reconcile to himself all things, whether on earth or in heaven, making peace by the blood of his cross.*

Perhaps we should not try to understand. Perhaps we should be like little children who run away from home (but not out of sight of the familiar red barn!) after a misdeed or quarrel with a parent and come home repentant to total forgiveness and total love and understand nothing but the laughter and the hugs and start all over to be happy again. Or like that older child, that young and younger son who left home (far from the sight of the familiar red barn), and after many misdeeds and quarreling with his better self came to himself—that is, to a broken and a contrite heart—and came home again to open arms and hugs and laughter. And that was absolutely *all* the father expected him to understand. And when the older son asked for an explanation, he was told quite simply: "It was fitting to make merry and be glad, for this your brother was dead, and is alive; he was lost, and is found."

# 6 THE EASTERING ASCENT

Amazingly and unexpectedly and quite appropriately, at the very time my thoughts had arrived at this final chapter, my husband and I had another underground experience. It had been 39 years since we entered that door in an ancient wall around a castle ruin in Germany, descended a quarter of a mile down flights of damp and crumbling steps, only to find at the end a barred exit. Now we made another descent by winding stairs, this time to an underground labyrinth of caves, the Caves of Drache on the Spanish island of Mallorca in the Mediterranean. This time our underground was splendidly and esthetically illuminated by electricity, and we made the journey in the company of a human throng of Spaniards, Germans, Danes, Swedes, Norwegians, Finns, as well as French, English, Irish, and Scotch tourists. In my ragbag of amazement clichés I find none adequate to describe these grottoes. The word "fantastic" shrinks to a cheap, tinsel word!

At the deepest depth of the Caves of Drache, under a vault of stalactites, lies a lake 177 meters long, 40 meters wide, and 3 meters deep. Deep down there we visitors to this underground wonder sat in a high-ceilinged natural auditorium and listened to a concert. The lights were turned out. At the far end of the lake we saw three boats (lit so we saw the boats' outlines but not the silent boat men) gliding toward us across the still water. In the middle boat, two unseen musicians, a cellist and a violinist, played as the boats glided past us and disappeared around huge pillars of stalagmites, only to turn silently and gracefully glide back again.

Appropriately, the music was slow, sonorous, and Lenten. We recognized Grieg. His music is universally known, so we were not surprised. But then, to our amazement, the unseen musicians began playing Ole Bull's music for Jørgen Moe's *"Seterjentens Søndag"!* Deep down in that Mallorcan cave, our ears heard the strains of the song of the Norwegian seter girl standing alone, high on a mountainside on a Sunday morning, tending the cattle and goats and listening to the church bells ringing in the valley below. Longing to be together with her family worshiping in the little country church. Longing to hear the old thanksgivings for daily blessings and the old supplications for their continuance. Longing to hear the ancient collects which she had heard so often, perhaps wearily, but now remembered so vividly and freshly. Longing to chant with her family and neighbors that most ancient of Christian liturgical prayers: Christ, thou Lamb of God, that taketh away the sins of the world. Longing to kneel at the altar with the humble family of God and receive his body and his blood.

In Walker Percy's *Love in the Ruins,* the protagonist, pondering his fallen, broken nature, asks, "What if man could re-enter paradise, so to speak, and live there both as man and spirit, whole and intact man-spirit, as solid flesh as a speckled trout, a dappled thing, yet aware of itself as a self!" The glory of the Christian faith is that it proclaims that a shattered person can be made whole again by the blood of Christ, more conjunctive and more indissoluble than the strongest glue. And that these two disjunctives, body and spirit, can be sutured by the surgery of the cross.

Will the seams show? They will, indeed—as long as we are residents of this earth. And there will always be the dark blue blemishes of new falls and the bright and bloodred thread of new redemptions. But we are intact! And we are whole! And a patchwork quilt is a lovely and a laughing thing. Its blithe and buoyant beauty is the beauty of ragbag scraps recovered and stitched and cross-stitched into a new whole.

The beauty of dappled things is celebrated in Gerard

Manley Hopkins' poem, "Pied Beauty," where he gives glory to God

> *For skies of couple-colour as a brinded cow;*
> *For rose-moles all in stipple upon trout that swim;*
> *Fresh-firecoal chestnuts-falls; finches' wings;*
> *Landscape plotted and pierced—fold, fallow, and*
> *plough. . . .*

But Hopkins does not mention in this poem the pied beauty of redeemed humanity, the kaleidoscopic beauty of the Easter man and the Easter woman, resurrected to possibility. Not the once-born or twice-born person, but the person who is continually being re-born.

How would the painter's eye see the person who has taken the descending path to the deepest depth of his fallen nature, has stood humbled, broken, and contrite before the broken body on the cross, and has returned on the ascending Easter path? A blind British poet who has made that journey asked himself that question as he sat for a painting of himself. If and when in a distant gallery a stranger stopped to gaze at the artist's portrait of him, "seeking the stark truth of my face," would "the flame break through?" "Marooned and fog-bound on the familiar chair" in his home-cottage, the poet sits a rigid hour for the painter and in his reflection speaks with him.

> *The snaky mist*
> *Has tunnelled down from a past so grim,*
> *A fate so drab, a painter could limn*
> *With Hogarth-smirch, Picasso-twist,*
> *Yet not belie the pervert brow,*
> *The humped will in the twilight. And what now?*

*You paint a man reborn through creed.*
*Pile on flamboyant colour: show my soul*
*Retrieved from the dead grey mask!*
*Bring Van Gogh riot to the task:*
*No wistful half-tones or granite glooms*
*Transmit the winged control.*

*Its bold rough bubbly light you need*
*To catch my spirit, trace the swerve*
*Away from the ego's fumes*
*And the tense blackened nerve.*
*The faithful lines will glow*
*With the convert's passion: you'll create*
*A hint of something shattered, and that's my fate.*

JACK CLEMO
"The Veiled Sitter"

"Pile on flamboyant color. . . . Bring Van Gogh riot to the task!" Well-spoken, for Van Gogh is indeed the Johann Sebastian Bach of art, the painter who truly saw the depths and the heights of humanity. Van Gogh was able to splash on canvas in bold colors and bubbly light the sometimes tortured but sublime synthesis of body and spirit that is humanity. His painter's eye saw humanity as that marvelous creation in which the world of eternity meets the world of time and space. His painter's eye saw that this marvelous meeting takes place in the humblest peasant—perhaps meets more readily there, for there is no wall of intellectual or spiritual pride to obstruct the meeting. Van Gogh painted human flesh as a sanctuary of sacred energy. Thus it is that his paintings invite us into the mystery of being human, of being redeemed humans.

"There is something noble," he wrote to his brother

Theo, "something that cannot be destined for the worms." Again, he wrote, "I should like to paint in men and women something of that quality of eternity which was symboled formerly by a halo and which we try to convey by the very radiance of our coloring."

Having taken the Lenten path to the very bottom, where all people ultimately know themselves to be mortal, vulnerable, and broken, having taken the path on which no one perishes because it leads to the Christ on the cross, Van Gogh could know resurrection joy and paschal exultation, and project the blinding light from his soul into his paintings. It was this paschal light in his soul that made him love the flaming sun of southern France. "Those who don't believe in the sun are real infidels," he wrote to Theo. The sun in Van Gogh's paintings roars that he himself was no infidel about either the sun or the Son. One wishes that whoever presided at the simple burial after Van Gogh's tragic death had read these lines from John Donne's "Hymn to God the Father."

*Swear by Thyself that at my death Thy Son*
*Shall shine as He shines now, and heretofore;*
*And, having done that, Thou hast done,*
*I fear no more.*

So, then—if I reach the bottom of the Lenten path and recognize my need for God's forgiving grace and do truly repent—then I ascend? I leap, I soar? Into the jonquil-yellow life a'glow and live there forever and forevermore? A legitimate citizen of the Kingdom A'glow, now that I have passed through the Kingdom A'shudder? The descending Lenten road may now be closed? If not for thee, at least for me? Closed for all time to the traffic of me?

"One gets used to everything in the long run," said Colonel Nicobar of the British Army of Occupation in the British Zone of Austria. He spoke to Schwester Kasimira, a nun, peeling potatoes "to the greater glory of God."

> *"Perhaps that is the tragedy of things," Schwester Kasimira said. "One gets used even to sanctifying grace. What one really needs is a new little conversion every day, a fresh bright light inside oneself to make one anxious to light fresh bright lights in other people. Perhaps that's what our Lord meant when He said that there was more joy in heaven over one sinner that repenteth than about all those who keep His commandments. Perhaps that's why the workers who came into the vineyard at the eleventh hour are paid the same wages as those who have borne the heat and burden of the day: because they have enthusiasm in their souls."*
>
> BRUCE MARSHALL
> *Vespers in Vienna*

It is true, miraculously true, that I am now a forgiven daughter, and that I am exuberant in the reconciliation with my divine Father. My sun flames in a clear-blue sky. I literally am newborn, a new creation, a new Eve. But I am still a human daughter of a human Eve as well as of a divine Father, and my chief enemy is still the I of myself. The I of myself is still my own worst enemy, for in the self of me there is still a human will (and how I do thank my God for the freedom of using it!).

In the a'glow of awareness of forgiveness and reconciliation, I pray "Thy will be mine," but I am still a mortal being, still capable of disobedience, of being self-willed. I, the loved and forgiven daughter who broke my Father's heart, will break my Father's heart again. And again and again. And as I, his loved and forgiven daughter, learn to know his will more clearly and more personally, I will find more subtle and hidden disobediences within me. I will sin again, I will sin new sins, and I will have to face the consequences of my sins. And as I learn to know and to love more truly him in whose image I am created, how can I not be a'shudder at how *un*like him I still am! At the same time, how can I help not striving all the more to be like him?

However, I now know from my own experience that there is no sin, no human condition, which cannot be forgiven when the sinner comes in contrition to the foot of the cross. I now rest in forgiveness, rest in God. As Søren Kierkegaard so beautifully expressed it, "A person rests in forgiveness when the thought of God does not remind him of sin but that he is forgiven, when the past is not a memory of how much he trespassed but of how much he has been forgiven." I rest, too, in the confidence that there is no experience, be it a my-fault, your-fault, or no-fault experience, that can either surprise me or crush me. There is no depth into which I may descend out of which I cannot by the grace of God ascend. Hosea had that confidence in the Lord of the old covenant:

> *Come, let us return to the Lord;*
> *for he has torn, that he may heal us;*
> *he has stricken, and he will bind us up . . .*
> *that we may live before him.*
> *Let us know, let us press on to know the Lord;*

*his going forth is sure as the dawn;*
*he will come to us as the showers,*
*as the spring rains that water the earth.*

My God has written a new covenant with humanity and signed it with his own redred blood, for he and his Son are one. I cannot understand it, but it is a fact of experience and it resurrects me from any and all my deaths.

This, then, is the change that the victorious, transcending power of Christ's death on the cross and his resurrection effects in me!

Changed—yes, *yes!* And yet unchanged. Still mortal! Still vulnerable! A mortal being with double citizenship —in God's kingdom and in the world, and the world is still the same old world. Its laws still operate the same as before. In the world of nature there are still earthquakes, tidal waves, tornadoes, typhoons, hurricanes, blizzards, fires, floods, snow slides, mud slides, droughts. Cancer still grows, ulcers gnaw, contagious diseases are still contagious, poison ivy and nettles are still to be avoided. In the world of humans there are still all the shocking catastrophes that are consequent to a fallen nature. Innocent little girls are still raped and murdered. Helpless old people are beaten and robbed. Who knows how many people in the world are being tortured—people whose only crime is to be against the powers that be. The rich get richer, the poor get poorer. Politicians are still all too human, and there are sure to be more Teapot Dome and Koreagate scandals. The human psyche will go right on playing emotional tricks on you and on me and will fetch up out of the subconscious into the conscious strange creatures we did not even know were there. You and I will still at times feel lonely, for loneliness is an existential condition. You and I will still fail and feel it, be discouraged and know it. You and I will hurt and be hurt, will wound and be wounded. And even in our life in the Spirit we are bound at times to have dry periods and feel *nothing,* and will have to rest in the creed of our Christian faith, be held in it—until the feelings dance again.

In short, we have ascended, but not into the life of absolute beatitude. In fact, I wonder if our polluted human natures—even if it were possible—are capable of enjoying a life of unpolluted beatitude here on earth!

In other better words, far better words than mine:

> *Skies will grow darker yet*
> *But the men signed with the Cross of Christ*
> *Go gaily in the dark.*
>
> G. K. CHESTERTON
> "The Ballad of the White Horse"

On the Lenten road to the bottom of myself, I discover how alien and unlike my fallen nature is to God's. At the foot of the cross I find atonement, at-one-ment. But I discover something else there as well. Down there at the bottom of myself I discover that *I am just like every other human being.* In my fallen nature, *un*like God but *like* all other human beings. I am not stranger and alien to them. Alien and unlike my God, but twin sister of my fellow men. I am at one with them in all my susceptibility and suggestibility in opposite directions and in all the consequences of my choices. We are united in all the pain and suffering of living in this world. We are united in causing much of it, for there is no "worldly evil." There is only the evil I, you, *we* introduce into this world. Down there at the bottom of me I am different from no other being. We are one. Fellow sinners. Fellow sufferers.

But how different we are up on the horizontal level of our existences! There we collect and accumulate differences, identify ourselves by our differences, cherish and adore our differences, become snobbish about them, group ourselves according to them, guard and defend our differences against those who envy and hate them. On the horizontal level of existence, it almost seems as if people *are* their differences. We are women or men before we are human beings. We are our skins, our IQs, our talents or untalents, our family status or unstatus, before we are members of the human race. It seems as if we clutch our accidental differences, identify with them, and march through life to the grave with them. The same holds true of the differences we acquire by culture and education. We are our jobs and professions. We are successes or failures, prosperous or poor.

Ah, some of us are even our particular religious persuasion before we are fully human, but if a religious persuasion has any quality at all it should provide us with an unflinchingly realistic picture of what it is to be a fully human being at one's best and at one's worst. It should reveal the social solidarity of original sin and the communion of sinners as well as the uniqueness of being a sanctuary of divine and eternal spirit and the communion of saints. Down at the bottom of the Lenten path, our uniqueness is that we are all uniquely the same. Down here the differences of prettiness, prominence, and popularity make no difference at all. We are all broken. We are all weak. Our kinship is in our weakness.

Paradoxically, there is a liberation and Easter resurrection in this insight gained at the end of the Lenten road. We are freed not only from the burden of our guilt, but also from the burden of our differences. We thank God that, having died to our selves and risen again in Christ, we are freed to become more like him. We thank God that fundamentally we are like all other humans. We are one with God again and one with all our fellow creatures. And now the door is wide open for the soul's response to this encounter with God's grace. Now, in the energizing power of Christ's Spirit, we celebrate the two liberations in twofold ways. We live our lives in Christ and in gratitude strive to become more like him. We live our lives for others and labor to participate in their sufferings. "Through him we have obtained access to this grace in which we stand, and we rejoice in our hope of sharing the glory of God" (Rom. 5:2).

> *But we have this treasure in earthen vessels, to show that the transcendent power belongs to God and not to us. We are afflicted in every way, but not crushed; perplexed, but not driven to despair; persecuted, but not forsaken; struck down, but not destroyed; always carrying in the body the death of Jesus, so that the life of Jesus may also be manifested in our bodies (2 Cor. 4:7-11).*

Now God's saving grace reaches out to our twofold effort—to be more like Christ, to be Christ's to others—and grace and effort go hand in hand in our lives. Grace stretches its hand to compassion, and the two walk side by side in our daily existences. But grace is not always an easy companion and does not aim to be. Life in the spirit is still life lived in a complex world and is filled with moral tension. Moreover, we live now with peeled eyeballs. As someone—I don't remember who—has said: Our hearts continue to be broken, but now they are broken by things that break the heart of God.

There may even be times when we fervently wish that we had not taken the Lenten road and that our spirits had been allowed to go on sleeping. Indeed, the rigors of this new life could never be endured without the support of prayer, without a constant interior turning to Jesus Christ. And since the most important fruit of prayer is contrition, we are constantly being reborn. Hence we are not once-born or twice-born. In this eternal process of being and becoming, we are not just born again but are born again and again and again. Thus every day in every way Scripture, the gospel, the Christian dogma—those old-fashioned truths!—are verified in me, in my flesh, and in its secret war with spirit!

Is Lent too long? Do the "saved" no longer need Lent? Ah, if the church fathers had not had the wisdom to put Lent into the church year and to teach it as essential to the Christian experience, the Christian faith would be totally inadequate to the complexity of life in this world. We would have mushy, marshmallow souls. The blood of our belief would be anemic. We would live in such spiritual vagueness and vapidity that we would become dreadfully indifferent to both our divine and our human natures. Indeed, our spirits very likely would become shriveled and useless appendages.

Thanks to the wisdom of the fathers and their listening to the counseling of the Spirit, we have a robust faith and the possibility of growing robust and vigorous souls. There is no evil that will surprise us, for knowing our own selves as we do we are painfully aware that people are not gods and earth is not heaven. There is no joy that will not take us by surprise, for we have opened our spirits to the Spirit of the Possible.

"Of course I want a robust, red-blooded soul, but, but—!" someone may still persistently protest. "Having once descended into the haunted house of my self, having once taken that nightmarish journey, do I really have to go again?" The questioner minimizes the power of evil and thinks it has used up all its resources on one's soul, forgetting that evil is infinitely resourceful and has had centuries in which to practice. Forgetting that culture and cultivation and the increase of knowledge are no impediments to evil. As the 20th, the most "enlightened" of centuries, so well illustrates, some of the grossest wickedness and suffering ever effected in human history has been effected by the most informed and sophisticated minds. As a matter of fact, the more advanced and sophisticated in knowledge we become, the more necessary it is for the good of our souls to make the descent that ascends.

But it is no longer a nightmarish journey into the labyrinth of the mind where one meets fear and death at every twist and turn. There has been an Eastering down there, too, and it is no longer a brooding, self-pitying, self-reviling place where one is neurotically conscious of nothing but disappointments, failures, and defects. For now the dark cave of self is illuminated by the light of the Spirit. Hence no evil we discover down there surprises or frightens us.

Lent, then, is the church's invitation to make a pilgrimage to Easter by the downward path. For the person who accepts the church's invitation, Lent becomes an annual pilgrimage into the depths of self. "Back down the slough / To Adam's sin-burnt calcinated bones," as we at the beginning of this book quoted from the poet Brother Antoninus's poem "The Making of the Cross." The same poet, in "The Kiss of the Cross," has also written the perfect lines with which to end this book for the Lenten pilgrim:

*I came*
*up out of darkness*
*deep holes and recesses,*
*black wells and cisterns of the self—*
*I came!*
*I came!*